STERLING

The Rescue of a Baby Harbor Seal

A NEW ENGLAND AQUARIUM BOOK
by Sandra Verrill White and Michael Filisky

Crown Publishers, Inc.   *New York*

Published by Crown Publishers, Inc., 225 Park Avenue South, New York, New York 10003

CROWN is a trademark of Crown Publishers, Inc.

Manufactured in Japan

Library of Congress Cataloging-in-Publication Data

White, Sandra Verrill.
Sterling: the rescue of a baby harbor seal
by Sandra Verrill White and Michael Filisky.
"A New England Aquarium book."
Summary: Text and photographs follow the story of an abandoned Harbor seal pup who is rescued and cared for at the New England Aquarium until she is strong enough to return to her natural environment.
1. Sterling (Seal)—Juvenile literature.   2. Wildlife rescue—Maine—Juvenile literature.   3. New England Aquarium Corporation—Juvenile literature.   4. Seals (Animals)—Maine—Biography. [1. Sterling (Seal) 2. Harbor seal.   3. Seals (Animals)   4. Wildlife rescue.]
I. Filisky, Michael, 1947-.   II. Title.
QL795.S43W48   1989
639.9′79748—dc19   88-16185
ISBN 0-517-57112-9   CIP
                                                            AC
10 9 8 7 6 5 4 3 2 1

First Edition

PHOTO CREDITS

Page 6 (top left): photograph copyright © 1986 by Catherine M. Allen

Page 6 (top right, bottom): photographs copyright © 1988 by Animals, Animals

Front jacket, pages 1, 9 (bottom), 10 (middle left, bottom left, bottom right), 11, 12, 13: photographs copyright © 1988 by Leslie Cowperthwaite

Pages 8, 9 (top): photographs copyright © 1987 by Andrew Martinez

Pages 4, 5, 7, 10 (top), 32, back jacket: photographs copyright © 1988 by Bruce M. Wellman

All other photos © 1987 by Kenneth Mallory and Margaret Thompson

ACKNOWLEDGMENTS

Greg Early, Associate Curator of Animal Care, New England Aquarium; Jeanne Rankin, formerly Librarian, New England Aquarium; The National Marine Fisheries Service, Portland, Maine; Barbara Ameen, Eastern Express Airlines

To the volunteers of the Marine Mammal Stranding Program at the New England Aquarium and of the Marine Mammal Stranding Network in Maine

In the cold ocean off the coast of New England, an
animal has come to the surface. What kind of animal
is it? It is a seal. In fact, it is the most common kind of seal
found in New England. It is a harbor seal.

Harbor seals are different from other northern seals. Gray seals like this fuzzy pup have much longer, horselike faces.

Hooded seals are much larger than harbor seals. Hooded seal pups have a beautiful dark back and cream-colored belly.

Harp seals, which are dark as adults, give birth to snow-white pups.

But only the harbor seals live in New England in large numbers. Several thousand of them make their homes off the coast of Maine.

A harbor seal hunts in the water and rests on the rocks by the shore. Its earholes and nostrils close tight to keep out icy waters; its large eyes and sensitive whiskers help it search the rocks for signs of food.

The harbor seal shares its underwater habitat with many kinds of animals and plants. Dense mats of rockweeds sway in the current. Periwinkle snails and prickly sea urchins graze on the seaweeds, while starfish search for tasty mussels. None of these tempt harbor seals.

Schools of small, silvery fish swim among the rocks and seaweeds. Usually, harbor seals try to catch slower-swimming fish than these.

A seal decides to come out of the water. Carefully, it hauls itself out onto the rocks that have been exposed by the outgoing tide.

This seal is a female, heavy with her first pup. She has come out of the water to give birth.

Away from other seals, the new pup comes into the world. Mother and pup touch noses and call to each other, learning each other's smells and sounds. Briefly, the pup nurses on her mother's rich milk and sleeps by her side.

The newborn follows her mother into the ocean. Newborn harbor seal pups have little insulating fat, so they cannot stay long in the chilly water. The pup returns to the beach to wait in the sun while her mother feeds in the sea. In a few days the pup's bright red birth cord will dry and fall off.

After several hours alone, the pup becomes hungry. She looks expectantly toward the sea, but there is no sign of her mother. Soon the harbor seal pup becomes distressed and calls softly.

By morning the pup is frantic for food. Several days later the mother seal has still not appeared. Dazed and weak, the pup wanders from the rocks to the beach.

Every spring on the coast of New England people find baby seals. Some of the pups have been orphaned, but most mother seals have just gone on short fishing trips. Fortunately, people also find signs like this one.

Someone from the Marine Mammal Stranding Network must determine that the little seal has really been abandoned.

The Marine Mammal Stranding coordinator sees how thin the pup is and knows this means the pup is probably a real orphan. The pup is immediately brought to the Animal Care Facility at the New England Aquarium.

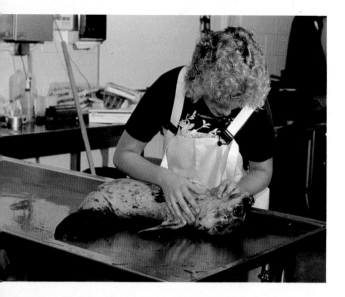

At the New England Aquarium the pup is placed on a steel examining table in a clean, bright room. Animal-care specialists check her temperature, weigh her, test her reflexes, and note her activity. The pup watches but is too weak to move.

Everything about the harbor seal pup is recorded on her own chart. To identify her a temporary tag is glued to the hair on her head. Every orphaned pup is given a name. Like most pups, she lost her very pale newborn coat a few days after birth. But because she still has a silvery sheen to her fur, she is called Sterling.

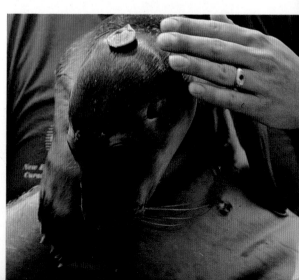

Sterling is placed in the
holding area, where other
pups snooze under the
warm lamps. She nuzzles
up to them and falls asleep.

Waking up, Sterling hears the voices of the keepers as they prepare infant seal formula. Making formula is messy work. Pounds of herring are filleted, then pureed in a blender. This fish mush is added to heavy cream, vegetable oil, vitamins, and minerals until it is the consistency of a thin milk shake. A portion is measured out for each pup and warmed before feeding.

Sterling is so thin that the keepers are very worried. If they can't get plenty of the nourishing formula into her stomach, Sterling will not live long. Sick seal pups find it difficult to nurse from a bottle. To feed Sterling, a flexible tube is inserted into her mouth and gently guided into her stomach. In only minutes her stomach is full.

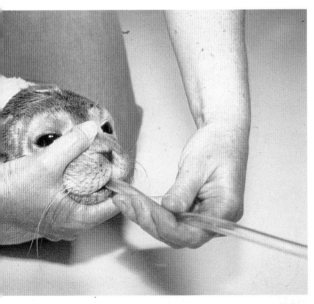

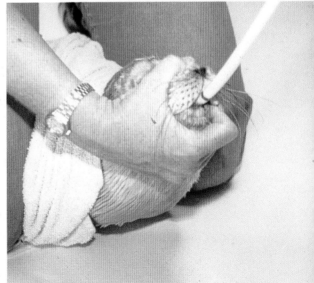

After the feedings, the keepers make notes about each pup and clean the pen with antiseptics. Their hunger satisfied, the pups sleep contentedly.

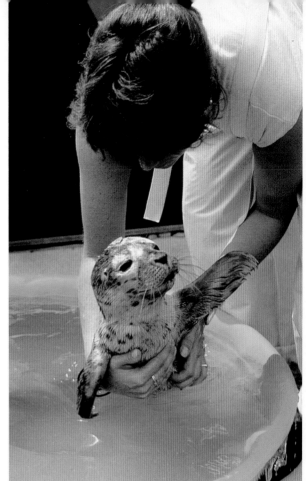

Later in the day, most of the pups follow the keepers around, begging for food and attention. Exercise is important for recovering seal pups, but when Sterling is introduced to the seal pup "swimming pool," she is too weak to play or swim. She flops out and wriggles onto a keeper's lap.

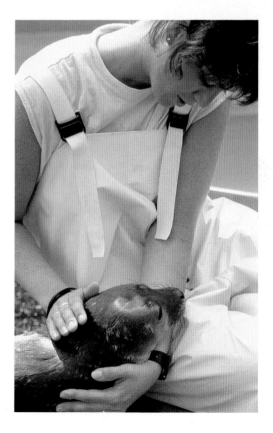

In several weeks, Sterling has put on weight
and grown teeth. If the keepers aren't careful,
they can get nipped. After all, Sterling is still
a wild harbor seal.

As the pups get stronger, they become more independent of the keepers. The little seals sleep and play together as a group. A daily swim helps prepare them for life in the ocean.

One day the keepers place some thawed fish in the pool to interest the pups in solid food. The pups nudge the fish around, biting at them. They are great playthings.

The seal pups play with the fish for
several days. Then, one afternoon the
pups are especially hungry. Sterling takes
a fish into the water. She holds it briefly
in her mouth and then swallows it whole.
Sterling has "caught" her first meal.

It doesn't take the other pups long to catch on to feeding and, when they learn how to eat fish, it seems they enjoy eating better than anything.

After two months, most of the pups have tripled their birth weight. They are swimming and eating just like adults. The time has come for their release into the wild.

Two pups are ready for release. One of them is Sterling. They are taken by van to the coast of Maine, where a colony of harbor seals has been spotted.

When the cages are opened Sterling dashes right into the water. The other pup is timid and carefully slides into the waves. In a few days the seals will lose their tags in the water.

Eventually both pups are so far away the keepers can't tell them apart from the wild seals. The rescued orphans are on their own.

There are many dangers in the sea for a young harbor seal. Sharks and other predators are always a threat. In recent years, however, dangers made by man have become very serious: chemical pollution, crowded harbors, garbage dumped in the sea.

People can cause problems for seals, but people can help, too. At the New England Aquarium, the Marine Mammal Stranding Network learns important facts about wild seals and their rehabilitation. This kind of knowledge could someday help save endangered seal species, such as the Hawaiian monk seal. The rescue of Sterling and the other baby harbor seals helps ensure there will always be wild animals in the waters of the world.